A GARDENER'S MISCELLANY

Edited by Diana Ajjan

Ariel Books

Andrews and McMeel

Kansas City

Frontispiece: Raundsclifffe—Everywhere Are Roses, 1906, George Samuel Elgood
Title page: Rosa Indica, Rosa Hemisphaerica from Choix des Plus Belles Fleurs, 1827-33. Pierre Joseph Redouté

The text of this book was set in Poetica Chancery by M space, Brooklyn, New York

Book design by Maura Fadden Rosenthal

ISBN: 0-8362-4735-3

·

ART CREDITS: half title: Prima Auricula (Bear's Ear) from Choix des Plus Belles Fleurs, 1827-33, Pierre Joseph Redouté; p.6: Summer 1917, Harold Harvey; p.8: A Nocturne, c.1885, John La Farge; pp. 10-11: A Summer Herbaceous Border, n.d., Lilian Stannard; p.12: Basket of Flowers (detail), n.d. Eugéne Delacroix; p.14: A Herbaceous Border, n.d., Hugh L. Norris; p.16: A Garden in France, 1879, John Lavery; p.20: Curcuma Roscoeana from Plantae Asiaticae Rariores, 1830-32, Nathaniel Wallich; p.23: Eugenia Bifaria (Clove) from Plantae Asiaticae Rariores, 1830-32, Nathaniel Wallich; p. 24: Nightingale (detail from a fresco Casa del Bracciale d'Oro, Pompeii), 1 AD; .24-25: Cottage Garden, Warwick, England (detail), n.d., Edmund H. Garrett, pp.30-31: In the Pleasaunce, Knostrop Old Hall, Leeds, n.d., John Atkinson Grimshaw; p.36: The Botanic Garden, c.1835, Benjamin Maund; pp.38-39: Blyborough, Lincolnshire, 1901, George Samuel Elgood; p.40: The Garden Path, n.d., Ernest Walbourn

A GARDENER'S MISCELLANY

CONTENTS

Introduction

THE LIFE OF A GARDENER

Awake and outdoors at daybreak, scurrying to finish a task before dark or rain, feeling the sun on your back or the cold March wind up your sleeve, hearing the soft patter of raindrops on your hat . . . such is the life of a gardener. A gardener is willing to get down on all fours, to sit on cool damp turf, to dig deep into the rich earth with fingers and hands. Neither squeamish at the sight of a worm nor afraid of the sting of a bee, the gardener has a healthy respect for the wildlife that shares his land.

A gardener is an artist as well as a scientist, developing over the years an eye for designing open spaces and combining the colors, shapes, and fragrances of trees, shrubs, hedges, and plants. A gardener also becomes familiar with the natural life cycle of plants, and learns how the conditions of soil and climate contribute to the success or failure of what grows (or doesn't grow) in the garden.

Not every gardener is marked by callused hands, sunburned cheeks, and an aching back. Many are limited to nothing more than a sunny city balcony or a thin slip of earth between two buildings, but they are gardeners nonetheless—lavishing the same care, affection, and imagination on their small plots as the ones who enjoy a wider terrain, and with shovel and hoe work tirelessly to create the gardens that flourish so vividly in their minds' eyes.

Gardening is a solitary and often meditative activity and for many gardeners the garden becomes a place of refuge—a private, even sacred spot where the cycle of the seasons is the only clock and time unfolds in a natural and unhurried way. Although gardeners may work from dawn till dusk—composting the soil, weeding the perennials, setting out plants, fighting the pests, bemoaning the weather—in the end, the peace and contentment they derive from creating even a small patch of beauty is immeasurable.

FLOWERS AND FRAGRANCE

Sunshine Blooms

ake a walk through a field of wildflowers or an overgrown meadow and your eyes will be dazzled by color. Buttery yellow, violet, orange, indigo, fuchsia, delicate pink, petals so blue they seem to reflect the sky . . . nature's true colors are a delight to behold.

The same radiant array of colors can be created in almost any sunny garden. The festive blooms of hydrangeas, foxgloves, coneflowers, peonies, lilies, irises, dragon flowers, hibiscus, delphinium, daisies, and clematis are just a few of the infinite varieties available to the flower gardener. No matter which color scheme you prefer in your garden—whether it be strictly whites and creams or the opulent display of the rainbow—you will find flowers and shrubs to delight your eye (and nose) in every season.

And remember, plants can be trained to climb fences or porch railings, to trail from window boxes, or to creep along the ground, so no matter how you envision your garden, you can usually find a plant whose growing habits will be a perfect match for your ideal.

Shady Hues

Noon doze,
wall cool against
my feet.
—Basho (tr. Lucien Stryk)

A shady garden on a hot summer day is a sensual oasis. And shade doesn't have to mean just green—great splashes of color can thrive under trees or along the sheltered side of your home. Colorful shade-loving blooms include periwinkle, hardy geraniums, gloxinia, lady's-mantle, honeybells, hosta, lily of the valley, daylilies, bleeding hearts, astilbe, hardy cyclamen, Virginia bluebells, hardy primrose, forget-me-nots, and violas.

The Sweet Smell of Success

Sweet, delicate, earthy, musky, bitter … the sundry fragrances in a garden beckon you to enter. The scent of flowers along a walkway provides a welcome greeting to visitors; and perhaps the aroma from your garden may drift away on the breeze—a serendipitous delight for your neighbors or others out for a stroll. Fragrance emanates not only from flowers but also from roots, bark, leaves, and stalks. Gardens smell sweetest when the weather is mild and somewhat humid; heat and drought stifle delicate scents. When you plant a garden, try to imagine the bouquet of the plants and flowers you choose. Avoid planting two strong-smelling varieties in close proximity;

they'll fight for attention and drown each other out. Instead, combine the sweet scent of lilacs with the fresh one of tulips, or the bold fragrance of the rose with the soft aroma of alyssum.

Fragrant spring blooms include lily of the valley, lilacs, narcissi, and jonquils. Some of the many flowers that blossom in the summer months include roses, irises, honeysuckle, daylilies, and sweet peas. Though the fragrance in a garden tends to decrease at the height of summer, scented flowers like clematis, butterfly bushes, hollyhocks, and hibiscus bloom well into autumn.

Garden scents can linger deep into the night, and some flowers only begin to bloom as dusk descends. Evening primroses, wisteria, and night-blooming jasmine save themselves for a wonderful evening display of color and scent. The night-blooming cereus, whose flowers fade and drop to the ground by dawn, is particularly delightful. So is the oversized Victoria Regia water lily whose blossoms open at dusk and close at dawn.

The Garden in a Vase

It is a joy to look out over a garden in full bloom and see the glorious result of all your hard work and planning. But it is equally delightful to bring part of your garden indoors: nothing brightens a room like a vaseful of fresh cut flowers. To prolong the life of cut flowers try the following: Pick flowers early in the morning, before the sun has a chance to sap their strength. Cut the flower stems on an angle, using a sharp knife or garden shears. Strip off the leaves so that none are in the vase, and use tepid water. If the stem is woody, split it about one inch up from the base; if the stems hold a lot of liquid, dip them in salt water after cutting the flowers. Change the water in the vase every day and snip the stems every other day. Some people claim that an aspirin tablet added to the water keeps the flowers fresher longer.

THE LANGUAGE OF FLOWERS

 bouquet can be a love letter, a sympathy note, a subtle reprimand, or a mixed message. Whatever you want to say, you can say it with flowers:

Acacia: friendship

Amaryllis: respect

Aster: loyalty

Carnation: steadfastness

Iris: dashed hopes

Lavender: sweet memories

Lilac: young love

Lily (white): innocence

Lupine: infatuation

Narcissus: vanity

Nasturtium: lost love

Peony: dignity

Poppy: indolence

Rose (red): earthly love

Rose (white): spiritual love

Rose (yellow): jealousy

Snapdragon: revenge

Sunflower: happiness

Violet: modesty

GARDEN WILDLIFE

September sunshine...
The hovering dragonfly's
Simmering shadow.
—Karo

our garden provides food and shelter to butterflies, bees, and birds. Hummingbirds and butterflies are attracted by bright-colored blossoms and thrive on the sweet nectar at the heart of these blooms. Birds of many varieties seek nesting nooks high in the treetops (or low in the shrubs), and bees are essential for the pollination of many flowers.

Trumpet vines, with their brilliant reddish-orange trumpet-shaped blossoms, attract hummingbirds like no other plant. The deep-purple fragrant blooms of the butterfly bush hold the same attraction for these sheer-winged insects. Other flowering plants that will lure hummingbirds and butterflies into the garden are red magic daylilies, pink coreopsis, white coneflowers, orange glory flowers, sweet William, and belladonna blue delphinium.

Place a birdhouse or birdbath in your garden (beyond the reach of cats or other predators) and cardinals, robins, bluebirds, orioles, grosbeaks, mockingbirds, blue jays, finches, scarlet tanagers, and cedar waxwings and warblers will reward you with a visit. Keep in mind that a lawn is no different from a meadow to a bird, and those birds that feed on flying insects will find the area above your lawn a smorgasbord of bugs. Remember, too, that the seeds of sunflowers and other flowering plants will provide food for the birds well into fall, so don't be in a hurry to cut back all those dead blossoms if you want birds to linger in your garden.

Sit quietly in your garden and you will hear the chirp of crickets and katydids, and the constant drone of bees. Your garden is host to beetles, grasshoppers, spiders, ants, worms, slugs, moles, moths, mice, chipmunks, caterpillars, gophers, frogs, and dragonflies. Depending on where you live, you might even receive some larger visitors (whether they are welcome or not), like Canadian geese, woodchucks, bats, snakes, raccoons, weasels, wild turkeys, pheasants, deer, and red foxes—even a black bear!

HERBAL DELIGHTS

n herb garden is not only pleasing to the senses of sight and smell, but it has many practical purposes. Nothing compares to using herbs fresh from your own garden for spicing up a recipe or drying herbs for potpourris, flower arrangements, and fragrant baths. Historically, herbal gardens were formal, symmetrically designed plots that featured intertwining hedges to separate the planted areas. Viewed from a terrace or window high above, they were as delightful to behold as any floral garden.

You can plant a similar decorative herbal garden or simply arrange your herbs in rows or clusters. A circular garden, with one herb at the hub and other herbs planted around it, makes a pleasing design.

Harvesting Your Herbs

Harvest your herbs just before they flower by cutting the stalks. Tie bunches of stems together and hang them upside down to dry, preferably in a dry place out of direct sunlight. You can also dry herbs by stripping the leaves and spreading them on a screen or rack. Turn the leaves to make sure that they dry completely. You'll know your herbs are dried when they become brittle to the touch. Store your dried herbs in tightly covered jars in a cool dry place.

Some common herbs for your kitchen garden are dill, savory, parsley, basil, oregano, tarragon, bay leaves, coriander, marjoram, fennel, thyme, rosemary, mint, sage, chervil, and chives.

In addition to the culinary herbs, you may plant the following to enhance wreaths, sachets, potpourris, and bath scents: lavender, santolina, scented geranium, lemon balm, bee balm, woodruff, and artemisia. For color highlights, you may want to plant statice, cornflowers, yarrow, and globe amaranth. And remember the rose—its dried petals add lovely scent and soft color to almost any mixture.

Herbs in the Kitchen

The most delightful way to enjoy your herb garden is to use fresh herbs for flavoring. Here are a few simple suggestions to get you started in the kitchen:

Herb Butter

Mix one or two tablespoons of chopped, fresh herbs (basil, tarragon, thyme, oregano) into half a cup of softened butter and season with salt and pepper. Use the herb butter as a sauce for pasta, or a baste for grilled meats, vegetables, or fish.

Garnishes and Flavorings

Mint is a versatile herb. Add fresh mint leaves to vanilla ice cream for a cool summer treat, or plop a fresh sprig into a cup of iced or hot tea.

Try stuffing a roasting chicken with a couple of handfuls of mint and a lemon poked with a fork. The lemony mint fragrance will permeate your kitchen as well as the roasting bird.

Pesto

Using a processor, blender, or mortar and pestle, mix about 2 1/2 cups of basil, 3 garlic cloves, 1/2 teaspoon of salt, and 1/2 cup of olive oil. Pour sauce over 1 pound of fresh or dried pasta and sprinkle with Parmesan cheese. Make a fresh green salad (from your vegetable garden) and you have a delicious, quick, and satisfying meal.

Herb Vinegars

Pick your herbs (dill, basil, tarragon, or rosemary) early in the morning, before the hot sun diminishes their aromatic oils. Place the herbs in a glass or ceramic container. Heat the vinegar (either cider or white wine), pour it over the herbs, and let it sit overnight. Strain the vinegar, put one or more fresh sprigs of herbs in a clean bottle, and fill the bottle with the flavored vinegar.

HERBAL POTPOURRIS

 lowers and herbs have been used throughout the ages to scent rooms, closets, drawers, linens, clothing, and even bodies. You can make your own potpourris by cutting flowers and herbs fresh from your garden and drying them. You can even include dried lemon, orange, and lime peels to add a fruity aroma. Try mixing different combinations of dried ingredients, including ground spices like cinnamon, cloves, or nutmeg, and extracts or oils to enhance the fragrance.

Lavender Potpourri

Gently mix the following in a ceramic or glass bowl:

> 1 ounce lavender
>
> 1/2 ounce wormwood
>
> 3 ounces thyme
>
> 1 teaspoon crushed cloves
>
> 1/2 ounce rosemary
>
> 1 teaspoon powdered orrisroot
>
> 1/4 ounce mint
>
> 1/4 ounce tansy

Leave the potpourri in the ceramic dish or sew it up into pleasing sachets to nestle among your lingerie or linens.

Fresh Scent Potpourri

Mix equal amounts (4 or 5 oz.) of marjoram, lavender, rosemary, and rosebuds, and equal amounts (1 oz.) of pennyroyal leaves, bergamot petals, and sage leaves. Add an ounce of orrisroot and a few drops of bergamot oil to enhance the scent.

Herbal Baths

Soaking in a steamy herbal bath is a wonderful way to start or end your day. There are several ways to prepare an herbal bath. You can boil the herbs (about a cup) in water for fifteen minutes, strain, and add the liquid to your bath; you can put the herbs directly into your bath water, though you'll need to clean them from your tub when you're through; or you can tie the herbs into a cloth bag and place this under the running spigot, and then float it in the bath water afterward.

Try mixing different amounts of various herbs to discover pleasing combinations. Useful herbs include orange, lemon, and strawberry leaves, mint, chamomile, lavender, rose, pennyroyal, sage, rosemary, thyme, eucalyptus leaves, patchouli, borage, passionflower, calamus, valerian, linden, and white willow bark.

SPEAKING OF GARDENS

All my hurts
My garden spade can heal.
—*Ralph Waldo Emerson*

Yes, in the poor man's garden grow
Far more than herbs and flowers—
Kind thoughts, contentment, peace of mind,
And joy for weary hours.
—*Mary Howitt*

I have a garden of my own
But so with roses overgrown
And lilies, that you would it guess
To be a little wilderness.
—*Andrew Marvell*

To dig one's own spade into one's own earth! Has life anything better to offer than this?
—Beverley Nichols

When I go into my garden with a spade, and dig a bed, I feel such an exhilaration and health that I discover that I have been defrauding myself all this time in letting others do for me what I should have done with my own hands.
—Ralph Waldo Emerson

In order to live off a garden, you practically have to live in it.
—Frank McKinney Hubbard

I will arise and go now, and go to Innisfree,
And a small cabin build there, of clay and wattles made:
Nine bean-rows will I have there, a hive for the honeybee,
And live alone in the bee-loud glade.
—W. B. Yeats

Every flower about a house certifies to the refinement of somebody. Every vine climbing and blossoming tells of love and joy.

—Robert G. Ingersoll

As I work among my flowers, I find myself talking to them, reasoning and remonstrating with them, and adoring them as if they were human beings. Much laughter I provoke among my friends by so doing, but that is of no consequence. We are on such good terms, my flowers and I!

—Celia Thaxter

A morning-glory at my window satisfies me more than the metaphysics of books.

—Walt Whitman

What a man needs in gardening is a cast-iron back, with a hinge in it.

—Charles Dudley Warner

The trouble with gardening is that it does not remain an avocation. It becomes an obsession.

–Phyllis McGinley

Old gardeners never die. They just spade away and then throw in the trowel.

–Herbert V. Prochnow

I know that if odour were visible, as colour is, I'd see the summer garden in rainbow clouds.

–Robert Bridges

One of the most delightful things about a garden is the anticipation it provides.

–W. E. Johns

To dig and delve in nice clean dirt
Can do a mortal little hurt.

–John Kendrick Bangs

Each spring ... a gardening instinct, sure as the sap rising in the trees, stirs within us. We look about and decide to tame another little bit of ground.

—Lewis Gannett

Earth laughs in flowers.

—Ralph Waldo Emerson

Life begins the day you start a garden.

—Chinese Proverb

One plant in a tin can may be a more helpful and inspiring garden to some mind than a whole acre of lawn and flowers may be to another ...

—Liberty Hyde Bailey

Gardens are our link with the divine.

—William Howard Adams

I love old gardens best—
tired old gardens
that rest in the sun.
–Henry Bellaman

One should learn also to enjoy the neighbor's garden, however
small; the roses struggling over the fence, the scent of lilacs
drifting across the road.
–Henry Van Dyke

When skies are blue and days are bright
A kitchen-garden's my delight,
Set round with rows of decent box
And blowsy girls of hollyhocks.
–Katharine Tynan

It is good to be alone in a garden at dawn or dark so that all its
shy presences may haunt you and possess you in a reverie of
suspended thought.
–James Douglas

If you once loved a garden
That love will stay with you.
—Louise Driscoll

Gardening is a habit of which I hope never to be cured, one
shared with an array of fascinating people who helped me
grow and bloom among my flowers.
—Martha Smith

When I walk out of my house into my garden I walk out of
my habitual self, my every-day thoughts, my customariness of
joy or sorrow by which I recognize and assure myself of my
own identity. These I leave behind me for a time, as the bather
leaves his garments on the beach.
—Alexander Smith

I have never had so many good ideas day after day as when I
worked in the garden.
—John Erskine

There are fairies at the bottom of our garden!

—Rose Fyleman

The greatest gift of a garden is the restoration of the five senses.

—Hanna Rion

O, what delights to us the garden ground doth bring?
Seed, leaf, flower, fruit, herb, bee, and tree, and more than
I may sing.

—Nicholas Grimaed

I am still devoted to the garden. But although an old man
I am but a young gardener.

—Thomas Jefferson

I perhaps owe having become a painter to flowers.

—Claude Monet

Perhaps no word of six letters concentrates so much satisfaction as the word "garden."

–Richard Le Gallienne

The scents of plants are like unseen ghosts. They sneak upon you as you round a turn in the garden, before you can see the plants from which they came.

–Barbara Damrosch

What is a weed? A plant whose virtues have not yet been discovered.

–Ralph Waldo Emerson

Gardens are not made by singing "Oh, how beautiful," and sitting in the shade.

–Rudyard Kipling

Here at my feet what wonders pass,
What endless, active life is here!
What blowing daisies, fragrant grass!

—Matthew Arnold

All through the long winter I dream of my garden. On the
first warm day of spring I dig my fingers deep into the soft
earth. I can feel its energy, and my spirits soar.

—Helen Hayes

Oh, little rose tree, bloom!
Summer is nearly over.
The dahlias bleed, and the phlox is seed.
Nothing's left of the clover.
And the path of the poppy no one knows.
I would blossom if I were a rose.

—Edna St. Vincent Millay

Daffodils,
That come before the swallow dares, and take
The winds of March with beauty.
—William Shakespeare

Last night, there came a frost, which has done great damage to
my garden.... It is sad that Nature will play such tricks with
us poor mortals, inviting us with sunny smiles to confide in
her, and then, when we are entirely within her power, striking
us to the heart.
—Nathaniel Hawthorne

Is there a joy except gardening that asks so much, and gives so
much? I know of no other except, perhaps, the writing of a
poem. They are much alike, even in the amount of waste that
has to be accepted for the sake of the rare, chancy joy when all
goes well.
—May Sarton

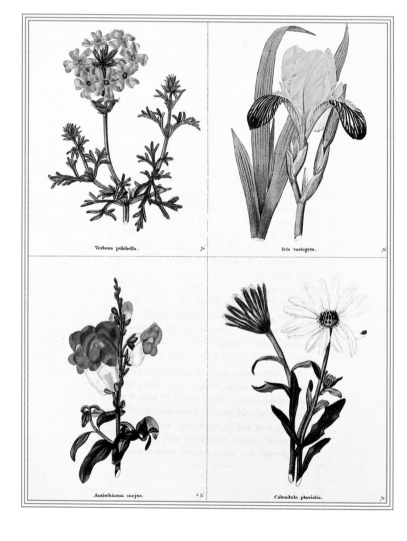

Verbena pulchella.

Iris variegata.

Antirrhinum majus.

Calendula pluvialis.

GARDEN FOLKLORE

 ebuchadnezzar was said to have built the Hanging Gardens of Babylon to appease his new bride, who longed for the lush hilly homeland she had left behind. Four acres of terraces, thickly planted with trees, shrubs, and flowers, were constructed to create the image of a mountain. Historians dispute whether the remains were indeed gardens or a fortress. Perhaps the proof that the Hanging Gardens of Babylon once existed can be demonstrated by later gardens that closely resembled those that Nebuchadnezzar reputedly built for his homesick bride.

Believing that asters were made from star dust and that they were sacred, the early Romans placed these flowers in all of the temples of the gods.

Every garden in the ancient Middle East had a cypress tree, which represented death, and an almond or plum tree, which symbolized life and hope.

The "flowery meade," or flower-filled lawn, was a favorite place in the Middle Ages for strolling and resting. People so enjoyed sitting on soft grassy patches, that they often built benches with natural turf seats.

The popularity of tulips blossomed in Holland in the 1630s. Scores of variations were cultivated and the prices of bulbs soared. It was a thriving market for both the aristocracy and commoners alike, with trade in bulbs expanding into a year-round activity. At the height of this craze, the cost of a single tulip bulb would be something like:

> 2 barrels of beer
> 2 hogshead of wine
> 2 barrels of butter
> 1,000 pounds of cheese
> 2 loads of wheat and 4 loads of rye
> A dozen sheep
> Several hefty oxen and pigs
> A piece of fine silver
> A room's set of furniture

… a pretty steep price to pay for just one tulip bulb!

Long ago, periwinkle was a favorite essential ingredient in love potions. It was also believed to ward off evil spirits.

The ancient art of aromatherapy, or using scents to treat both emotional and physical ills, has been practiced since medieval times. Violets were among the first flowers considered useful both for cooking and for medicinal purposes. Here are some of the specific herbs and flowers whose aromas were believed to alleviate specific symptoms:

Basil: to stimulate the heart and relieve melancholy

Rosemary: to preserve youth

Marjoram: to help relieve melancholy

Garlic: to protect against infection when eaten or carried

Thyme: to raise the spirits and increase energy

Mint: to refresh the spirit

Violets: to aid digestion and dispel sadness.

An old English legend has it that lily-of-the-valley blooms sprouted wherever drops of blood had fallen upon the ground from St. George, who had to battle a fierce fire-breathing dragon.

In colonial times, people filled bags with marigolds and kept them near fireplaces or chimneys to dry out so that they could be used as curatives. The leaves were inhaled to cure a head cold, and yellow dye was made from the flowers to use as hair coloring. Marigolds were also thought to be a cure for toothaches, moles, and warts, and they were steeped in wine as a relief for stomach aches.

In addition to using sunflowers for cooking, American settlers in the 1800s planted the giant flowers around their houses in the belief that they would protect them from malaria.

The sarsaparilla herb rose to fame in the early 1960s because of a television show called "Sugarfoot." The main character of the program had a habit of ordering a sarsaparilla at the local tavern, and this became a popular soft drink at the time.

The biblical legend of lavender says that Mary hung the infant Jesus' clothes on a lavender bush to dry. When she returned to get them, the bushes smelled sweetly of the fragrance as we know it today.

In contrast to this gentle legend, the ancient Egyptians believed that the viper that killed Cleopatra was hiding under a lavender bush. Lavender, therefore, became a symbol of distrust.